Artificial Intelligence for
Quantum Machine Learning

COPYRIGHTS

Disclaimer

The information provided in this book is for general informational purposes only. While we have made every attempt to ensure that the information contained in this book is accurate and up-to-date, the author and publisher make no representations or warranties of any kind, express or implied, about the completeness, accuracy, reliability, suitability, or availability with respect to the book or the information, products, services, or related graphics contained in the book for any purpose. Any reliance you place on such information is therefore strictly at your own risk.

In no event will the author or publisher be liable for any loss or damage including without limitation, indirect or consequential loss or damage, or any loss or damage whatsoever arising from loss of data or profits arising out of, or in connection with, the use of this book.

The views and opinions expressed in this book are those of the author and do not necessarily reflect the official policy or position of any other agency, organization, employer, or company. Assumptions made in this book are not reflective of the position of any entity other than the author, and since we are critically-thinking human beings, these views are always subject to change, revision, and rethinking at any time.

Table of Contents

Introduction

Overview of Artificial Intelligence (AI) and Quantum Computing

Artificial Intelligence: Artificial Intelligence (AI) is a branch of computer science focused on creating systems capable of performing tasks that typically require human intelligence. These tasks include learning, reasoning, problem-solving, perception, language understanding, and more. AI can be broadly categorized into narrow AI, which is designed for a specific task, and general AI, which aims to perform any intellectual task that a human can. Key milestones in AI development include the creation of expert systems in the 1970s, the rise of machine learning in the 1990s, and the recent advancements in deep learning.

Quantum Computing: Quantum computing leverages the principles of quantum mechanics to process information in fundamentally different ways than classical computers. Classical computers use bits as the basic unit of information, represented as either 0 or 1. Quantum computers use quantum bits (qubits), which can exist in superposition states, representing both 0 and 1 simultaneously. Additionally, qubits can be entangled, allowing quantum computers to perform complex computations more efficiently than classical computers. Key concepts in quantum computing include quantum gates, quantum circuits, and quantum algorithms.

The Intersection of AI and Quantum Computing: Quantum Machine Learning (QML)

Quantum Machine Learning (QML): Quantum Machine Learning is an emerging interdisciplinary field combining the principles of quantum computing with machine learning algorithms. QML aims to leverage the computational power of quantum computers to enhance the capabilities of traditional machine learning techniques. By utilizing the unique properties of qubits, such as superposition and entanglement, QML algorithms can potentially solve certain problems faster and more efficiently than classical algorithms.

Potential of QML: The potential of QML lies in its ability to tackle complex problems that are currently intractable for classical computers. This includes optimization problems, large-scale data analysis, and simulating quantum systems. QML can provide significant speed-ups for tasks like training deep learning models, performing large-scale optimization, and executing high-dimensional data analysis. As quantum hardware continues to evolve, the potential applications of QML will expand, offering transformative solutions across various industries.

Importance and Potential of QML in Modern Technology

Accelerating Machine Learning: QML has the potential to revolutionize the field of machine learning by significantly accelerating the training and inference processes of complex models. Quantum-enhanced machine learning algorithms can process large datasets more efficiently, leading to faster and more accurate predictions. This acceleration can be crucial for applications in fields such as healthcare, finance, and scientific research, where timely and accurate data analysis is essential.

Advancing Scientific Research: In scientific research, QML can be used to simulate quantum systems and solve complex problems in physics, chemistry, and biology. For instance, QML can help in the discovery of new materials, optimization of chemical reactions, and understanding of biological processes at the molecular level. These advancements can lead to breakthroughs in drug discovery, materials science, and energy solutions.

Enhancing Cryptography and Security: Quantum computing poses both challenges and opportunities for cryptography and cybersecurity. While quantum computers have the potential to break current cryptographic protocols, QML can also be used to develop new quantum-resistant cryptographic algorithms. Furthermore, QML can enhance anomaly detection systems and improve cybersecurity measures by identifying patterns and threats more effectively.

Transforming Industries: The impact of QML extends to various industries, including finance, healthcare, logistics, and manufacturing. In finance, QML can optimize trading strategies, risk management, and fraud detection. In healthcare, QML can improve diagnostic accuracy, personalize treatment plans, and accelerate drug discovery. In logistics and manufacturing, QML can optimize supply chains, improve production efficiency, and enhance predictive maintenance.

Future Outlook: The future of QML is promising, with ongoing research and development aimed at overcoming current challenges and unlocking its full potential. As quantum hardware continues to advance, and more efficient QML algorithms are developed, the adoption of QML in real-world applications will increase. Collaborative efforts between academia, industry, and government will play a crucial role in driving the progress of QML and ensuring its successful integration into various sectors.

The intersection of artificial intelligence and quantum computing in the form of Quantum Machine Learning represents a groundbreaking advancement in technology. By harnessing the unique capabilities of quantum computers, QML has the potential to revolutionize machine learning and transform various industries. The importance of QML in modern technology cannot be overstated, as it offers solutions to complex problems that were previously thought to be unsolvable. As we continue to explore and develop this emerging field, the future of QML holds exciting possibilities for advancing science, enhancing industry processes, and improving the quality of life.

This introduction provides a comprehensive overview of the key concepts and significance of Quantum

Machine Learning, setting the stage for the detailed exploration in the subsequent chapters.

Chapter 1:

Foundations of Artificial Intelligence

Definition and History of AI

Definition of AI: Artificial Intelligence (AI) is a field of computer science dedicated to creating systems that can perform tasks typically requiring human intelligence. These tasks include reasoning, learning, problem-solving, perception, language understanding, and decision-making. AI can be broadly categorized into two types: Narrow AI, which is designed for specific tasks, and General AI, which aims to perform any intellectual task a human can.

History of AI: The history of AI can be traced back to ancient myths and stories about artificial beings endowed with intelligence. However, modern AI began in the mid-20th century with the development of electronic computers. Key milestones in the history of AI include:

1950s: Alan Turing proposed the Turing Test as a measure of machine intelligence. The Dartmouth Conference in 1956, organized by John McCarthy,

Marvin Minsky, Nathaniel Rochester, and Claude Shannon, is considered the birth of AI as a field of study.

1960s-1970s: The development of early AI programs such as ELIZA, a natural language processing program, and SHRDLU, a program capable of understanding and manipulating blocks in a virtual world.

1980s: The rise of expert systems, which used knowledge-based rules to simulate human expertise in specific domains. These systems were commercially successful but eventually faced limitations due to their rigidity and lack of learning capabilities.

1990s: The resurgence of AI with the advent of machine learning, particularly with algorithms that could learn from data rather than relying solely on predefined rules. The development of support vector machines (SVMs) and neural networks marked significant progress.

2000s-Present: The era of big data and increased computational power led to the rise of deep learning, a subfield of machine learning focused on neural networks with many layers. Major breakthroughs include the success of convolutional neural networks (CNNs) in image recognition and recurrent neural networks (RNNs) in natural language processing.

Key Concepts: Machine Learning, Deep Learning, Neural Networks

Machine Learning (ML): Machine learning is a subset of AI that involves the development of algorithms that allow computers to learn from and make predictions or decisions based on data. ML algorithms can be classified into three main types:

Supervised Learning: The algorithm is trained on a labeled dataset, meaning that each training example is paired with an output label. The goal is to learn a mapping from inputs to outputs that can be applied to new, unseen data. Common algorithms include linear regression, logistic regression, and support vector machines.

Unsupervised Learning: The algorithm is trained on an unlabeled dataset, meaning that it must find patterns or structures in the data without any predefined labels. Common techniques include clustering (e.g., k-means, hierarchical clustering) and dimensionality reduction (e.g., principal component analysis, t-SNE).

Reinforcement Learning: The algorithm learns by interacting with an environment and receiving feedback in the form of rewards or penalties. The goal is to learn a policy that maximizes cumulative rewards over time. Applications include game playing (e.g., AlphaGo) and robotics.

Deep Learning: Deep learning is a subfield of machine learning that focuses on neural networks with many layers (hence "deep"). These networks, known as deep neural networks (DNNs), are capable of learning complex representations of data. Key components of deep learning include:

Convolutional Neural Networks (CNNs): Designed for processing grid-like data such as images. CNNs use convolutional layers to automatically and adaptively learn spatial hierarchies of features from input images.
Recurrent Neural Networks (RNNs): Designed for sequential data such as time series or natural language. RNNs use feedback connections to process sequences of inputs, maintaining a memory of previous inputs in the sequence.
Generative Adversarial Networks (GANs): Consist of two neural networks, a generator and a discriminator, that are trained simultaneously. The generator creates fake data samples, while the discriminator tries to distinguish between real and fake samples. GANs are widely used in image generation, super-resolution, and other creative applications.

Neural Networks: Neural networks are the foundation of deep learning. They are computational models inspired by the human brain, consisting of interconnected nodes (neurons) organized into layers. Key components of neural networks include:

Neurons and Layers: Each neuron receives input, processes it using a weighted sum and an activation function, and passes the output to the next layer. Layers can be input layers, hidden layers, or output layers.

Activation Functions: Functions that introduce non-linearity into the network, allowing it to learn complex patterns. Common activation functions include sigmoid, tanh, and ReLU (rectified linear unit).

Training and Backpropagation: The process of training a neural network involves adjusting the weights of the connections between neurons to minimize the error between the predicted output and the true output. Backpropagation is an algorithm used to compute the gradients of the error with respect to the weights, which are then updated using gradient descent.

Major Breakthroughs and Current Trends in AI

Major Breakthroughs:

ImageNet Competition (2012): The success of AlexNet, a deep convolutional neural network, in the ImageNet Large Scale Visual Recognition Challenge demonstrated the power of deep learning for image classification.

AlphaGo (2016): Developed by DeepMind, AlphaGo defeated the world champion Go player, showcasing the potential of reinforcement learning and deep neural networks for complex strategic games.

GPT-3 (2020): OpenAI's Generative Pre-trained Transformer 3 (GPT-3) is a state-of-the-art language model capable of generating human-like text and performing a wide range of natural language processing tasks.

Current Trends:

Explainable AI (XAI): As AI systems become more complex, there is a growing need for transparency and interpretability. XAI aims to make AI decisions understandable to humans, enhancing trust and accountability.

AI Ethics and Fairness: Ensuring that AI systems are ethical, unbiased, and fair is a critical concern. Researchers and policymakers are developing guidelines and frameworks to address issues related to bias, privacy, and accountability.

Edge AI: The deployment of AI models on edge devices (e.g., smartphones, IoT devices) for real-time processing and reduced latency. Edge AI is driven by advancements in hardware and efficient model architectures.

AI in Healthcare: AI is revolutionizing healthcare through applications such as medical imaging, drug discovery, personalized treatment, and predictive analytics. The integration of AI in healthcare aims to improve patient outcomes and reduce costs.

AI for Climate Change: AI is being used to address climate change through applications such as climate modeling, energy optimization, and environmental monitoring. AI-driven solutions are essential for sustainable development and mitigating the impact of climate change.

Understanding the foundations of artificial intelligence is essential for grasping the complexities and potential of Quantum Machine Learning (QML). This chapter has provided a comprehensive overview of AI's definition, history, key concepts, and major breakthroughs. As we delve deeper into the intersection of AI and quantum computing, this foundational knowledge will serve as a crucial backdrop for exploring the transformative capabilities of QML in subsequent chapters.

This detailed chapter provides an in-depth exploration of the foundations of AI, setting the stage for the more advanced topics covered later in the book.

Chapter 2:

Basics of Quantum Computing

Introduction to Quantum Mechanics

Quantum Mechanics Overview: Quantum mechanics is a fundamental theory in physics that describes the behavior of particles at the atomic and subatomic levels. Unlike classical mechanics, which deals with macroscopic objects and predictable behaviors, quantum mechanics deals with the probabilistic nature of particles. The core principles of quantum mechanics include wave-particle duality, superposition, and entanglement.

Wave-Particle Duality: One of the fundamental concepts of quantum mechanics is wave-particle duality, which posits that particles such as electrons and photons exhibit both wave-like and particle-like properties. This duality is best illustrated by the double-slit experiment, where particles passing through two slits create an interference pattern characteristic of waves, yet they also behave like discrete particles.

Superposition: Superposition is the principle that a quantum system can exist in multiple states simultaneously until it is measured. For example, a quantum bit (qubit) can be in a state representing 0, 1, or any superposition of these states. Mathematically, a qubit's state can be represented as $|\psi\rangle = \alpha|0\rangle + \beta|1\rangle$, where α and β are complex numbers that determine the probability amplitudes of the states 0 and 1, respectively.

Entanglement: Entanglement is a quantum phenomenon where the states of two or more particles become correlated such that the state of one particle instantly determines the state of the other, regardless of the distance between them. Entanglement is a key resource in quantum computing, enabling phenomena like quantum teleportation and superdense coding.

Quantum Bits (Qubits) vs. Classical Bits

Classical Bits: In classical computing, the basic unit of information is the bit, which can take on one of two possible values: 0 or 1. Classical bits are the building blocks of classical computers, used in binary operations to perform calculations and store information.

Quantum Bits (Qubits): Qubits are the fundamental units of information in quantum computing. Unlike classical bits, qubits can exist in a superposition of states, representing both 0 and 1 simultaneously. This property allows quantum computers to process a vast amount of information in parallel, providing a significant advantage over classical computers for certain tasks.

Physical Realizations of Qubits: Qubits can be realized using various physical systems, including:

Superconducting Qubits: Utilized by companies like IBM and Google, these qubits are based on superconducting circuits cooled to extremely low temperatures.

Trapped Ions: Companies like IonQ and Honeywell use ions trapped in electromagnetic fields as qubits, manipulated using lasers.

Topological Qubits: Microsoft is exploring topological qubits, which use exotic quasiparticles called anyons that are less susceptible to errors.

Photonic Qubits: Photons can be used as qubits in optical quantum computing, taking advantage of their coherence and low interaction with the environment.

Quantum Superposition and Entanglement

Superposition in Depth: Superposition allows quantum computers to explore many possible solutions simultaneously. For a system with n qubits, the number of possible states is 2^n, leading to an exponential increase in computational power compared to classical systems. However, measuring a quantum state collapses it to one of the possible basis states, making it crucial to design algorithms that maximize the advantage of superposition before measurement.

Entanglement in Depth: Entanglement enables powerful correlations between qubits that classical bits cannot achieve. Entangled qubits exhibit non-local correlations, meaning the state of one qubit instantly affects the state of another, no matter the distance between them. This property is essential for many quantum algorithms and protocols, such as Shor's algorithm for factoring large numbers and Grover's algorithm for search problems.

Quantum Gates and Circuits

Quantum Gates: Quantum gates are the building blocks of quantum circuits, analogous to classical logic gates. They manipulate the state of qubits through unitary operations, which are reversible transformations that preserve the total probability of the system. Common quantum gates include:

Pauli-X Gate: Analogous to the classical NOT gate, it flips the state of a qubit from $|0\rangle$ to $|1\rangle$ and vice versa.

Hadamard Gate: Creates a superposition state from a basis state, transforming $|0\rangle$ to $(|0\rangle + |1\rangle)/\sqrt{2}$ and $|1\rangle$ to $(|0\rangle - |1\rangle)/\sqrt{2}$.

CNOT Gate: A two-qubit gate that flips the state of the target qubit if the control qubit is in the state $|1\rangle$.

Phase Gate: Applies a phase shift to the state of a qubit, useful for creating complex quantum states.

Quantum Circuits: Quantum circuits are sequences of quantum gates applied to qubits to perform computations. A quantum circuit can be represented by a quantum circuit diagram, where lines represent qubits, and gates are depicted as symbols along these lines. Quantum algorithms are implemented by designing specific quantum circuits that leverage superposition, entanglement, and interference to solve problems more efficiently than classical algorithms.

Universal Quantum Gates: A set of quantum gates is called universal if any quantum operation can be approximated to arbitrary precision using a finite sequence of these gates. The most common universal gate set includes the Hadamard gate, phase gate, and CNOT gate. These gates are sufficient to construct any quantum algorithm.

Quantum computing represents a paradigm shift in how we approach computation, leveraging the unique principles of quantum mechanics to perform tasks that are infeasible for classical computers. Understanding the basics of quantum mechanics, qubits, quantum superposition, entanglement, and quantum gates is essential for exploring the potential of quantum computing. This foundational knowledge sets the stage for delving into more advanced topics, including quantum algorithms and their applications in machine learning, which will be covered in subsequent chapters.

This comprehensive chapter provides an in-depth understanding of the basics of quantum computing, essential for grasping the more complex concepts and applications discussed later in the book.

Chapter 3:

Quantum Algorithms

Overview of Essential Quantum Algorithms

Quantum algorithms leverage the principles of quantum mechanics, such as superposition, entanglement, and interference, to solve certain computational problems more efficiently than classical algorithms. Some of the most notable quantum algorithms include Grover's algorithm, Shor's algorithm, and the Quantum Fourier Transform (QFT). These algorithms demonstrate the potential of quantum computing to tackle complex problems in cryptography, search, and optimization.

Grover's Algorithm for Search Problems

Problem Statement: Grover's algorithm addresses the problem of searching an unsorted database of NNN items to find a specific item. Classically, this problem requires $O(N)O(N)O(N)$ time, as one would need to check each item in the worst case. Grover's algorithm, however, can solve this problem in $O(N)O(\sqrt{N})O(N)$ time, providing a quadratic speedup.

Algorithm Outline:

Initialization:

Prepare an initial state by applying the Hadamard gate to each qubit, creating an equal superposition of all possible states.

Oracle:

Use a quantum oracle to mark the correct solution. The oracle is a black box function that flips the amplitude of the correct solution.

Amplitude Amplification:

Apply Grover's diffusion operator to amplify the probability amplitude of the correct solution. This step involves reflecting the state about the mean amplitude.

Iteration:

Repeat the oracle and amplitude amplification steps $O(N)O(\sqrt{N})O(N)$ times to maximize the probability of measuring the correct solution.

Measurement:

Measure the quantum state to obtain the correct solution with high probability.

Quantum Circuit: The quantum circuit for Grover's algorithm consists of Hadamard gates, the quantum oracle, and the diffusion operator. The oracle is problem-specific and encodes the solution, while the diffusion operator can be implemented using Hadamard and Pauli-X gates.

Shor's Algorithm for Factoring

Problem Statement: Shor's algorithm solves the problem of integer factorization, which is the basis for the security of many cryptographic systems, such as RSA encryption. Classically, factoring large integers is computationally hard, requiring exponential time. Shor's algorithm can factor integers in polynomial time, posing a threat to current cryptographic protocols.

Algorithm Outline:

Quantum Period Finding:

The core of Shor's algorithm is the quantum period-finding subroutine, which determines the period of a function related to the factors of the integer NNN.

Initialization:

Prepare two quantum registers: one for the input values and another for storing the function values.

Superposition:

Apply the Hadamard gate to the input register to create a superposition of all possible input values.

Function Evaluation:
>Evaluate the function and store the results in the output register.

Quantum Fourier Transform (QFT):
>Apply the QFT to the input register to identify the period of the function.

Measurement:
>Measure the input register to obtain an approximation of the period, which can then be used to find the factors of NNN using classical post-processing.

Quantum Circuit: The quantum circuit for Shor's algorithm includes the QFT, controlled modular exponentiation, and measurement steps. The QFT is a key component, enabling the efficient extraction of the period.

Quantum Fourier Transform (QFT)

Concept: The Quantum Fourier Transform is the quantum analogue of the classical discrete Fourier transform (DFT). It transforms a quantum state from the computational basis to the frequency domain, enabling efficient solutions to problems such as period finding and phase estimation.

Mathematical Representation: For an nnn-qubit state $|x\rangle$|x\rangle|x\rangle, the QFT transforms it into:

$|y\rangle = \frac{1}{\sqrt{2^n}} \sum_{k=0}^{2^n-1} e^{2\pi i \frac{kx}{2^n}} |k\rangle$ |y\rangle =
\frac{1}{\sqrt{2^n}} \sum_{k=0}^{2^n-1} e^{2\pi i
\frac{kx}{2^n}} |k\rangle|y\rangle = \frac{1}{\sqrt{2^n}} \sum_{k=0}^{2^n-1}
$e^{2\pi i \frac{x}{2^n} k} |k\rangle$

Algorithm Outline:

Initialization:
> Start with an nnn-qubit quantum state.

Hadamard Gate:
> Apply the Hadamard gate to the first qubit to create superposition.

Controlled Phase Rotation:
> Apply controlled phase rotation gates to entangle the first qubit with the remaining qubits, introducing the appropriate phase shifts.

Repetition:
> Repeat the process for the remaining qubits, applying Hadamard gates and controlled phase rotations.

Swap Gates:
> Apply swap gates to reverse the order of the qubits, as the QFT reverses the order of the output bits.

Quantum Circuit: The QFT circuit consists of Hadamard gates, controlled phase rotations, and swap gates. The controlled phase rotations introduce the necessary phase shifts to transform the state into the frequency domain.

Other Notable Quantum Algorithms

Deutsch-Jozsa Algorithm: The Deutsch-Jozsa algorithm determines whether a given function is constant or balanced with only one evaluation, providing an exponential speedup over classical methods.

Quantum Phase Estimation: This algorithm estimates the phase (or eigenvalue) associated with an eigenvector of a unitary operator. It is a fundamental subroutine used in many quantum algorithms, including Shor's algorithm and the Quantum Approximate Optimization Algorithm (QAOA).

Variational Quantum Eigensolver (VQE): VQE is a hybrid quantum-classical algorithm used to find the ground state energy of a quantum system. It combines quantum circuits to prepare variational states with classical optimization routines to minimize the energy expectation value.

Quantum algorithms leverage the unique properties of quantum mechanics to solve certain computational problems more efficiently than classical algorithms.

Grover's algorithm provides a quadratic speedup for unstructured search problems, while Shor's algorithm offers an exponential speedup for integer factorization, threatening classical cryptographic systems. The Quantum Fourier Transform is a crucial component of many quantum algorithms, enabling efficient period finding and phase estimation. Understanding these essential quantum algorithms lays the foundation for exploring more advanced topics and applications in quantum machine learning and beyond.

This detailed chapter provides an in-depth exploration of essential quantum algorithms, offering insights into their workings, applications, and significance in the broader context of quantum computing and machine learning.

Chapter 4:

Introduction to Machine Learning

Overview of Machine Learning

Definition and Importance: Machine learning (ML) is a subset of artificial intelligence (AI) that focuses on developing algorithms and statistical models that enable computers to learn from and make decisions based on data. Unlike traditional programming, where rules and logic are explicitly coded, ML algorithms identify patterns and relationships within data to make predictions or decisions. The importance of ML spans various domains, from image and speech recognition to autonomous vehicles, finance, healthcare, and more.

Types of Machine Learning

Supervised Learning: In supervised learning, algorithms are trained on labeled datasets, where each input data point is paired with the correct output. The goal is to learn a mapping from inputs to outputs that can be applied to new, unseen data. Common supervised learning tasks include classification (e.g., spam detection) and regression (e.g., predicting house prices).

Key Algorithms:

Linear Regression: Models the relationship between a dependent variable and one or more independent variables using a linear equation.

Logistic Regression: Used for binary classification, estimating the probability that a given input belongs to a certain class.

Support Vector Machines (SVM): Finds the optimal hyperplane that separates data points of different classes with maximum margin.

Decision Trees and Random Forests: Tree-based models that split data into subsets based on feature values, with random forests combining multiple trees for better generalization.

Neural Networks: Composed of interconnected layers of neurons, capable of modeling complex relationships in data.

Unsupervised Learning: Unsupervised learning involves training algorithms on unlabeled data, where the goal is to discover hidden patterns or structures. Common tasks include clustering (e.g., grouping customers based on purchasing behavior) and dimensionality reduction (e.g., reducing the number of features while preserving important information).

Key Algorithms:

K-Means Clustering: Partitions data into K clusters based on feature similarity, iteratively refining the cluster centroids.

Hierarchical Clustering: Builds a tree-like structure of nested clusters, merging or splitting clusters based on distance metrics.

Principal Component Analysis (PCA): Reduces the dimensionality of data by projecting it onto the principal components that capture the most variance.

Autoencoders: Neural network-based models that learn efficient representations of data by training to reconstruct the input data.

Reinforcement Learning: Reinforcement learning (RL) involves training agents to make sequential decisions by interacting with an environment. Agents receive rewards or penalties based on their actions and learn to maximize cumulative rewards over time. RL is widely used in game playing, robotics, and autonomous systems.

Key Concepts:

Markov Decision Processes (MDPs): Mathematical framework for modeling decision-making, consisting of states, actions, transition probabilities, and rewards.

Policy: A strategy that defines the actions an agent should take in each state.

Value Function: Estimates the expected cumulative rewards from a given state or state-action pair.

Q-Learning: A model-free RL algorithm that learns the optimal action-value function, which estimates the value of taking an action in a given state.

Key Concepts in Machine Learning

Training and Testing:

Training: The process of fitting an ML model to a training dataset by adjusting the model's parameters to minimize the error or loss.

Testing: Evaluating the trained model's performance on a separate test dataset to assess its generalization ability.

Overfitting and Underfitting:

Overfitting: When a model learns the training data too well, capturing noise and irrelevant patterns, leading to poor performance on new data.

Underfitting: When a model is too simple to capture the underlying patterns in the data, resulting in poor performance on both training and test data.

Model Evaluation Metrics:

Accuracy: The proportion of correct predictions out of the total number of predictions, commonly used for classification tasks.

Precision and Recall: Precision measures the proportion of true positives among predicted positives, while recall measures the proportion of true positives among actual positives.

F1 Score: The harmonic mean of precision and recall, providing a balanced metric for imbalanced datasets.

Mean Squared Error (MSE): The average of the squared differences between predicted and actual values, commonly used for regression tasks.

Feature Engineering: The process of selecting, transforming, and creating features to improve model performance. This can involve techniques such as normalization, encoding categorical variables, and creating interaction terms.

Deep Learning and Neural Networks

Introduction to Deep Learning: Deep learning is a subset of ML that focuses on neural networks with many layers, known as deep neural networks (DNNs). These models can automatically learn hierarchical representations of data, making them highly effective for tasks such as image and speech recognition.

Key Components:

Neurons and Layers: The basic units of neural networks, where each neuron receives input, applies a weighted sum and an activation function, and passes the output to the next layer.

Activation Functions: Functions that introduce non-linearity into the network, enabling it to learn complex patterns. Common activation functions include ReLU (rectified linear unit), sigmoid, and tanh.

Loss Function: A function that measures the discrepancy between the predicted and actual values, guiding the optimization process. Common loss functions include cross-entropy for classification and MSE for regression.

Backpropagation: An algorithm used to compute the gradients of the loss function with respect to the network's weights, which are then updated using optimization techniques such as gradient descent.

Popular Architectures:

Convolutional Neural Networks (CNNs): Designed for processing grid-like data such as images, CNNs use convolutional layers to automatically learn spatial hierarchies of features.

Recurrent Neural Networks (RNNs): Designed for sequential data such as time series or natural language, RNNs use feedback connections to process sequences of inputs, maintaining a memory of previous inputs in the sequence.

Generative Adversarial Networks (GANs): Consist of two neural networks, a generator and a discriminator, trained simultaneously. The generator creates fake data samples, while the discriminator tries to distinguish between real and fake samples.

Recent Advances and Applications of Machine Learning

Natural Language Processing (NLP): NLP involves developing algorithms to process and understand human language. Recent advances include the development of transformer-based models like BERT and GPT, which have significantly improved performance on tasks such as text classification, machine translation, and question answering.

Computer Vision: Computer vision focuses on enabling computers to interpret and understand visual information from the world. Deep learning has revolutionized this field, with CNNs achieving state-of-the-art results in image classification, object detection, and image generation.

Healthcare: ML is transforming healthcare through applications such as medical image analysis, disease prediction, personalized treatment plans, and drug discovery. These advancements are improving diagnostic accuracy, patient outcomes, and treatment efficiency.

Autonomous Systems: ML is a critical component of autonomous systems, including self-driving cars, drones, and robots. These systems rely on ML algorithms for perception, decision-making, and control, enabling them to navigate complex environments and perform tasks autonomously.

Finance: In finance, ML is used for algorithmic trading, risk management, fraud detection, and customer service. ML models analyze large volumes of financial data to identify patterns, make predictions, and optimize investment strategies.

Machine learning is a rapidly evolving field with wide-ranging applications and transformative potential. Understanding the fundamentals of ML, including its types, key concepts, and recent advances, is essential for exploring its intersection with quantum computing. This chapter provides a comprehensive overview of ML, setting the stage for the integration of quantum computing and machine learning, which will be explored in subsequent chapters.

This comprehensive chapter provides an in-depth exploration of machine learning, offering insights into its types, key concepts, recent advances, and applications, essential for understanding the intersection with quantum computing.

Chapter 5:

Quantum Machine Learning Fundamentals

Introduction to Quantum Machine Learning (QML)

Definition and Scope: Quantum Machine Learning (QML) is an emerging interdisciplinary field that combines the principles of quantum computing with machine learning algorithms to enhance computational capabilities and address complex problems. QML aims to leverage quantum mechanics' unique properties, such as superposition, entanglement, and quantum parallelism, to improve the efficiency and performance of machine learning tasks.

Motivation: The motivation behind QML arises from the limitations of classical machine learning, particularly in dealing with large datasets and complex models. Quantum computers have the potential to process information exponentially faster than classical computers, making them suitable for handling large-scale data and computationally intensive tasks. By integrating quantum computing with machine learning, researchers aim to develop algorithms that can solve problems more efficiently and accurately.

Key Concepts in Quantum Machine Learning

Quantum Data: Quantum data refers to information that is represented and processed using quantum bits (qubits). Unlike classical data, which is binary and exists in distinct states of 0 or 1, quantum data can exist in multiple states simultaneously due to superposition. This enables quantum algorithms to explore and process a vast amount of information in parallel.

Quantum States and Vectors: Quantum states are mathematical representations of the state of a quantum system. In QML, quantum states are often represented as vectors in a high-dimensional complex vector space known as Hilbert space. The state of a qubit can be described by a two-dimensional vector, while the state of a system with multiple qubits can be represented by a higher-dimensional vector.

Quantum Operators: Quantum operators are mathematical functions that act on quantum states to transform them. In QML, quantum operators are used to manipulate qubits, perform measurements, and implement quantum gates. Common quantum operators include unitary transformations, which preserve the norm of quantum states, and Hermitian operators, which are used to measure observables.

Quantum Circuits: Quantum circuits are sequences of quantum gates applied to qubits to perform computations. In QML, quantum circuits are used to implement machine learning algorithms by encoding data into quantum states, applying quantum transformations, and measuring the output. Quantum circuits are represented using quantum circuit diagrams, where lines represent qubits and gates are depicted as symbols along these lines.

Quantum Machine Learning Models

Quantum Supervised Learning: In quantum supervised learning, algorithms are trained on labeled quantum data to learn a mapping from inputs to outputs. Quantum analogs of classical supervised learning algorithms, such as quantum support vector machines (QSVM) and quantum neural networks (QNN), have been developed to leverage the advantages of quantum computing.

Quantum Support Vector Machines (QSVM): QSVMs are quantum versions of classical support vector machines, which are used for classification tasks. QSVMs use quantum feature maps to encode classical data into high-dimensional quantum states, allowing for the separation of data points in a higher-dimensional space. Quantum algorithms are then used to find the optimal hyperplane that separates the data points with maximum margin.

Quantum Neural Networks (QNN): QNNs are neural networks implemented on quantum computers. QNNs consist of layers of quantum gates that act as neurons, with each layer performing a unitary transformation on the input quantum states. QNNs can model complex relationships in data and are used for tasks such as image recognition, natural language processing, and generative modeling.

Quantum Unsupervised Learning: In quantum unsupervised learning, algorithms are trained on unlabeled quantum data to discover hidden patterns or structures. Quantum versions of classical unsupervised learning algorithms, such as quantum clustering and quantum principal component analysis (QPCA), have been developed to leverage the advantages of quantum computing.

Quantum Clustering: Quantum clustering algorithms aim to partition quantum data into clusters based on similarity. Quantum k-means clustering is a quantum analog of the classical k-means algorithm, which iteratively assigns data points to clusters and updates the cluster centroids. Quantum clustering algorithms can potentially provide exponential speedups over classical algorithms by leveraging quantum parallelism.

Quantum Principal Component Analysis (QPCA): QPCA is a quantum version of the classical principal component analysis (PCA) algorithm, which is used for dimensionality reduction. QPCA leverages quantum algorithms to compute the principal components of quantum data, allowing for efficient extraction of the most significant features. QPCA can potentially provide exponential speedups over classical PCA by leveraging quantum parallelism.

Quantum Reinforcement Learning (QRL): In quantum reinforcement learning, agents are trained to make sequential decisions by interacting with a quantum environment. Quantum analogs of classical reinforcement learning algorithms, such as quantum Q-learning and quantum policy gradients, have been developed to leverage the advantages of quantum computing.

Quantum Q-Learning: Quantum Q-learning is a quantum version of the classical Q-learning algorithm, which is used for model-free reinforcement learning. Quantum Q-learning algorithms use quantum operators to update the Q-values, which represent the expected cumulative rewards for taking specific actions in given states. Quantum Q-learning can potentially provide speedups over classical Q-learning by leveraging quantum parallelism and entanglement.

Quantum Policy Gradients: Quantum policy gradient algorithms are quantum versions of classical policy gradient algorithms, which are used for policy-based reinforcement learning. Quantum policy gradient algorithms use quantum circuits to represent policies and update the policy parameters using quantum operators. Quantum policy gradients can potentially provide speedups over classical policy gradients by leveraging quantum parallelism and entanglement.

Implementing Quantum Machine Learning Algorithms

Quantum Data Encoding: One of the key challenges in QML is encoding classical data into quantum states. Various encoding techniques, such as amplitude encoding, basis encoding, and angle encoding, have been developed to represent classical data in quantum states. The choice of encoding technique depends on the nature of the data and the specific QML algorithm being used.

Amplitude Encoding: Amplitude encoding represents classical data as the amplitudes of quantum states. For example, a classical vector $[x_0, x_1, ..., x_{n-1}][x_0, x_1, ..., x_{n-1}][x_0, x_1, ..., x_{n-1}$

] can be encoded into a quantum state $\sum_{i=0}^{n-1} x_i |i\rangle$. Amplitude encoding allows for efficient representation of high-dimensional data, but it requires normalization of the data to ensure that the quantum state is valid.

Basis Encoding: Basis encoding represents classical data as the basis states of quantum states. For example, a classical binary vector $[x_0, x_1, ..., x_{n-1}]$ can be encoded into a quantum state $|x_0\rangle \otimes |x_1\rangle \otimes ... \otimes |x_{n-1}\rangle$. Basis encoding is simple and intuitive, but it requires a large number of qubits for high-dimensional data.

Angle Encoding: Angle encoding represents classical data as the angles of quantum states. For example, a classical vector $[x_0, x_1, ..., x_{n-1}]$ can be encoded into a quantum state $\prod_{i=0}^{n-1} R_y(x_i)|0\rangle$, where $R_y(x_i)$ is a rotation gate that rotates the state $|0\rangle$ by an angle x_i. Angle encoding is useful for representing continuous data, but it requires careful selection of the rotation angles to ensure that the quantum state is valid.

Challenges and Future Directions in Quantum Machine Learning

Scalability and Noise: One of the major challenges in QML is the scalability of quantum algorithms and the impact of noise on quantum computations. Current quantum computers, known as Noisy Intermediate-Scale Quantum (NISQ) devices, have a limited number of qubits and are prone to errors due to noise. Developing error-correcting codes and fault-tolerant quantum algorithms is crucial for the practical implementation of QML on larger scales.

Hybrid Quantum-Classical Algorithms: Hybrid quantum-classical algorithms combine the strengths of quantum and classical computing to overcome the limitations of current quantum hardware. In these algorithms, quantum circuits are used to perform specific subroutines, while classical computers handle the remaining computations. Hybrid algorithms, such as the Variational Quantum Eigensolver (VQE) and Quantum Approximate Optimization Algorithm (QAOA), have shown promise in solving complex optimization problems.

Algorithmic Advances: Continued research in QML is focused on developing new quantum algorithms and improving existing ones. This includes exploring new techniques for quantum data encoding, developing more efficient quantum circuits, and designing algorithms that can leverage the unique properties of quantum computing to achieve speedups over classical algorithms.

Applications and Use Cases: QML has the potential to revolutionize various fields, including drug discovery, materials science, finance, and cryptography. Identifying and developing practical use cases for QML is a key area of research, with the goal of demonstrating quantum advantage in real-world applications.

Quantum Machine Learning is a rapidly evolving field that holds the promise of transforming machine learning by leveraging the unique properties of quantum computing. Understanding the fundamentals of QML, including quantum data, quantum states, quantum operators, and quantum circuits, is essential for exploring its potential. This chapter provides a comprehensive overview of QML fundamentals, laying the groundwork for delving into more advanced topics and practical applications in subsequent chapters.

This detailed chapter provides an in-depth exploration of the fundamentals of Quantum Machine Learning, offering insights into its key concepts, models, implementation challenges, and future directions, essential for understanding the integration of quantum computing and machine learning.

Chapter 6:

Quantum Data Encoding Techniques

Introduction to Quantum Data Encoding

Definition and Importance: Quantum data encoding refers to the process of converting classical data into quantum states that can be processed by quantum algorithms. This is a crucial step in quantum machine learning (QML) because quantum computers operate on qubits and quantum states rather than classical bits. The efficiency and effectiveness of QML algorithms largely depend on how well the data is encoded into quantum states.

Challenges: The main challenges in quantum data encoding include ensuring that the encoded data preserves the essential features of the original data, managing the high-dimensional nature of quantum states, and efficiently preparing these states on current quantum hardware. Different encoding methods have been developed to address these challenges, each with its advantages and limitations.

Common Quantum Data Encoding Techniques

Amplitude Encoding:

Concept: Amplitude encoding represents classical data as the amplitudes of a quantum state. This method allows the encoding of a large amount of data into a relatively small number of qubits, making it highly efficient in terms of space.

Mathematical Representation: Given a classical vector $[x0,x1,...,xN-1][x\_0, x\_1, ..., x\_{N-1}][x0,x1,...,xN-1]$, amplitude encoding maps this vector to a quantum state $|\psi\rangle|\psi\rangle|\psi\rangle$ as follows: $|\psi\rangle = \sum_{i=0}^{N-1} x_i |i\rangle|\psi\rangle = \sum_{i=0}^{N-1} x_i |i\rangle$ where $|i\rangle|i\rangle|i\rangle$ represents the computational basis states of the qubits, and $x_i x\_i x_i$ are the corresponding amplitudes.

Advantages:

Efficiency: Amplitude encoding can represent NNN classical data points using only $\log_2(N)\log_2(N)\log_2(N)$ qubits.
Scalability: Suitable for high-dimensional data due to its logarithmic space complexity.

Limitations:

Normalization Requirement: The vector [x0,x1,...,xN−1][x_0, x_1, ..., x_{N-1}][x0,x1,...,xN−1] must be normalized to ensure that the resulting quantum state is valid, i.e.,

$$\sum_{i=0}^{N-1} |x_i|^2 = 1$$

$\sum$i=0N−1|xi|2=1.

State Preparation: Preparing the quantum state with specific amplitudes can be challenging and resource-intensive on current quantum hardware.

Basis Encoding:

Concept: Basis encoding, also known as computational basis encoding, represents classical data using the basis states of qubits. Each classical data point is mapped to a unique quantum state.

Mathematical Representation: Given a classical binary vector [x0,x1,...,xn−1][x_0, x_1, ..., x_{n-1}][x0,x1,...,xn−1], basis encoding maps this vector to a quantum state $|\psi\rangle$|ψ⟩ as follows:

$$|\psi\rangle = |x_0\rangle \otimes |x_1\rangle \otimes ... \otimes |x_{n-1}\rangle$$

|ψ⟩=|x0⟩⊗|x1⟩⊗...⊗|xn−1⟩ where

$\otimes$\otimes$\otimes$ denotes the tensor product, and $|xi\rangle$|x_i\rangle|xi\rangle are the basis states (0 or 1).

Advantages:

Simplicity: Basis encoding is straightforward to implement and does not require data normalization.
Direct Mapping: Each bit of the classical data directly corresponds to a qubit, making it intuitive.

Limitations:

Space Complexity: Basis encoding requires one qubit per bit of the classical data, leading to high space complexity for large datasets.
Limited Use: Primarily useful for binary data or data that can be naturally represented in a binary format.

Angle Encoding:

Concept: Angle encoding represents classical data as the angles of quantum states. This method uses rotation gates to encode data points into the quantum state.

Mathematical Representation: Given a classical vector $[x0,x1,...,xn-1]$[x_0, x_1, ..., x_{n-1}]$[x0,x1,...,xn-1]$, angle encoding maps this vector to a quantum state $|\psi\rangle$|\psi\rangle|\psi\rangle$ as follows:

$|\psi\rangle = \prod_{i=0}^{n-1} R_y(x_i)|0\rangle$|\psi\rangle =

\prod_{i=0}^{n-1} R_y(x_i) |0\rangle|ψ⟩=∏i=0n−1 Ry(xi)|0⟩ where Ry(xi)R_y(x_i)Ry(xi) is a rotation gate that rotates the state |0⟩|0\rangle|0⟩ by an angle xix_ixi.

Advantages:

Continuous Data Representation: Angle encoding is suitable for representing continuous data.
Flexibility: Can be adapted to encode various types of data by adjusting the rotation angles.

Limitations:

Gate Complexity: Requires a sequence of rotation gates for each data point, which can be resource-intensive.
Normalization: The angles must be carefully selected to ensure valid quantum states.

Advanced Quantum Data Encoding Techniques

Qubit Encoding:

Concept: Qubit encoding represents classical data using the states of individual qubits. This method often involves encoding data into the superposition states of qubits.

Mathematical Representation: Given a classical vector $[x_0, x_1, ..., x_{n-1}]$, qubit encoding maps this vector to a quantum state $|\psi\rangle$ as follows: $|\psi\rangle = \sum_{i=0}^{n-1} \alpha_i |q_i\rangle$ where α_i are coefficients, and $|q_i\rangle$ are the qubit states.

Advantages:

Parallelism: Leverages the parallelism of quantum states to encode multiple data points simultaneously.
Scalability: Suitable for encoding larger datasets into a smaller number of qubits.

Limitations:

Complexity: Requires careful preparation and manipulation of quantum states.
Error Sensitivity: More susceptible to errors due to the complex quantum state preparation.

Hybrid Encoding:

Concept: Hybrid encoding combines multiple encoding techniques to leverage their respective strengths. For example, a hybrid approach might use amplitude encoding for some features and angle encoding for others.

Mathematical Representation: Hybrid encoding combines different methods into a single quantum state, potentially represented as:
$|\psi\rangle = \sum_{i=0}^{N-1} \alpha_i R_y(x_i) |i\rangle$ where α_i are amplitude coefficients, and $R_y(x_i)$ are rotation gates.

Advantages:

Flexibility: Allows for customized encoding strategies based on the data characteristics.
Optimized Performance: Can optimize encoding to balance efficiency and accuracy.

Limitations:

Complex Implementation: Combining different encoding methods can increase the complexity of the quantum circuit.
Resource Intensive: May require more quantum resources, such as qubits and gates, compared to using a single encoding method.

Practical Considerations for Quantum Data Encoding

Data Preprocessing: Before encoding classical data into quantum states, it is often necessary to preprocess the data. Preprocessing steps may include normalization, scaling, and feature selection to ensure that the data is suitable for quantum encoding.

Quantum State Preparation: Preparing quantum states efficiently on current quantum hardware is a critical consideration. Researchers are developing algorithms and techniques to minimize the resources required for state preparation while maintaining the accuracy of the encoded data.

Error Mitigation: Quantum computations are prone to errors due to noise and decoherence. Implementing error mitigation strategies, such as error-correcting codes and noise reduction techniques, is essential to ensure the reliability of encoded quantum data.

Hardware Constraints: The choice of encoding method may be influenced by the limitations of the available quantum hardware. For example, certain encoding techniques may require a large number of qubits or complex quantum gates, which may not be feasible on current devices.

Quantum data encoding is a fundamental aspect of quantum machine learning, enabling the representation of classical data in quantum states. Various encoding techniques, including amplitude encoding, basis encoding, angle encoding, qubit encoding, and hybrid encoding, offer different advantages and challenges. Understanding these techniques and their practical considerations is essential for developing efficient and effective QML algorithms. This chapter provides a comprehensive overview of quantum data encoding techniques, laying the foundation for exploring more advanced QML topics in subsequent chapters.

This detailed chapter provides an in-depth exploration of quantum data encoding techniques, offering insights into their concepts, mathematical representations, advantages, limitations, and practical considerations. This knowledge is essential for effectively integrating quantum computing with machine learning.

Chapter 7:

Quantum Algorithms for Machine Learning

Introduction to Quantum Algorithms for Machine Learning

Definition and Importance: Quantum algorithms are computational procedures that leverage the principles of quantum mechanics to solve problems more efficiently than classical algorithms. In the context of machine learning (ML), quantum algorithms have the potential to significantly speed up computations and improve the performance of various ML tasks. The integration of quantum algorithms into machine learning can lead to breakthroughs in data processing, optimization, and pattern recognition.

Historical Context: The development of quantum algorithms for machine learning is rooted in the pioneering work of quantum computing and classical machine learning. Landmark quantum algorithms, such as Shor's algorithm for factoring and Grover's algorithm for unstructured search, have demonstrated the potential of quantum computing. Building on these foundations, researchers have been exploring how quantum principles can be applied to machine learning, resulting in the emergence of quantum machine learning (QML).

Key Quantum Algorithms for Machine Learning

Quantum Support Vector Machines (QSVMs):

Concept: Support Vector Machines (SVMs) are classical supervised learning algorithms used for classification and regression tasks. Quantum Support Vector Machines (QSVMs) leverage quantum computing to perform these tasks more efficiently, particularly in high-dimensional feature spaces.

Mathematical Framework: QSVMs use quantum feature maps to encode classical data into high-dimensional quantum states. The goal is to find a hyperplane that maximally separates different classes of data points in this high-dimensional space. The quantum kernel trick is used to compute the inner products of the quantum states efficiently.

Advantages:

High-Dimensional Mapping: QSVMs can map data to exponentially large feature spaces, making it easier to find separating hyperplanes.

Quantum Speedup: QSVMs can achieve significant speedups in training and inference compared to classical SVMs, particularly for large datasets.

Applications:

Image and speech recognition
Financial modeling
Bioinformatics

Quantum Principal Component Analysis (QPCA):

Concept: Principal Component Analysis (PCA) is a classical unsupervised learning algorithm used for dimensionality reduction. Quantum Principal Component Analysis (QPCA) leverages quantum computing to perform PCA more efficiently, particularly for large datasets.

Mathematical Framework: QPCA uses quantum algorithms to compute the principal components of a dataset. The goal is to find the eigenvectors corresponding to the largest eigenvalues of the data covariance matrix. Quantum phase estimation and other quantum algorithms are used to perform these computations efficiently.

Advantages:

Exponential Speedup: QPCA can achieve exponential speedups in computing principal components compared to classical PCA.

Handling Large Datasets: QPCA is particularly effective for high-dimensional data, where classical PCA becomes computationally infeasible.

Applications:

Data compression
Image and video processing
Anomaly detection

Quantum Clustering:

Concept: Clustering is a classical unsupervised learning task that involves partitioning data into groups based on similarity. Quantum clustering algorithms leverage quantum computing to perform clustering more efficiently and accurately.

Mathematical Framework: Quantum k-means clustering is a quantum version of the classical k-means algorithm. It uses quantum superposition and entanglement to explore multiple cluster assignments simultaneously. Quantum algorithms are used to compute distances and update cluster centroids efficiently.

Advantages:

Parallelism: Quantum clustering algorithms can explore multiple cluster assignments in parallel, leading to faster convergence.

Improved Accuracy: Quantum algorithms can achieve more accurate clustering by exploring a larger solution space.

Applications:

Market segmentation
Image segmentation
Document clustering

Quantum Neural Networks (QNNs):

Concept: Neural Networks (NNs) are classical supervised learning algorithms used for various tasks, including classification, regression, and generative modeling. Quantum Neural Networks (QNNs) leverage quantum computing to enhance the capabilities of neural networks.

Mathematical Framework: QNNs consist of layers of quantum gates that act as neurons. Each layer performs a unitary transformation on the input quantum states. Quantum backpropagation algorithms are used to train the network by updating the parameters of the quantum gates.

Advantages:

High Expressive Power: QNNs can represent complex functions more efficiently than classical NNs.

Quantum Speedup: QNNs can achieve significant speedups in training and inference, particularly for large networks and datasets.

Applications:

Image and speech recognition
Natural language processing
Generative modeling

Quantum Boltzmann Machines (QBMs):

Concept: Boltzmann Machines (BMs) are classical probabilistic graphical models used for generative modeling and unsupervised learning. Quantum Boltzmann Machines (QBMs) leverage quantum computing to enhance the capabilities of Boltzmann Machines.

Mathematical Framework: QBMs use quantum annealing and other quantum algorithms to sample from the Boltzmann distribution efficiently. The goal is to learn the probability distribution of the data by minimizing the difference between the model distribution and the data distribution.

Advantages:

Efficient Sampling: QBMs can sample from complex distributions more efficiently than classical BMs.

Enhanced Modeling: QBMs can model complex data distributions more accurately.

Applications:

Generative modeling
Pattern recognition
Data synthesis

Implementing Quantum Algorithms for Machine Learning

Quantum Circuits: Quantum circuits are used to implement quantum algorithms. A quantum circuit consists of qubits and quantum gates that manipulate these qubits to perform computations. Understanding the design and optimization of quantum circuits is crucial for implementing QML algorithms.

Quantum Gates: Quantum gates are the building blocks of quantum circuits. They perform unitary transformations on qubits, allowing for the manipulation of quantum states. Common quantum gates used in QML include Hadamard gates, Pauli gates, CNOT gates, and rotation gates.

Hybrid Quantum-Classical Algorithms: Hybrid quantum-classical algorithms combine the strengths of quantum and classical computing. In these algorithms, quantum circuits are used to perform specific subroutines, while classical computers handle the remaining computations. Examples of hybrid algorithms include the Variational Quantum Eigensolver (VQE) and Quantum Approximate Optimization Algorithm (QAOA).

Challenges and Future Directions

Hardware Limitations: Current quantum hardware, known as Noisy Intermediate-Scale Quantum (NISQ) devices, have limitations in terms of the number of qubits, gate fidelity, and error rates. Developing robust QML algorithms that can perform well on NISQ devices is a key challenge.

Algorithmic Complexity: Designing efficient quantum algorithms for machine learning involves overcoming the complexity of quantum state preparation, quantum operations, and measurement. Ongoing research is focused on developing algorithms that can leverage quantum speedup while minimizing resource requirements.

Scalability: Scaling QML algorithms to handle large datasets and complex models remains a challenge. Hybrid algorithms and error-correction techniques are being explored to improve the scalability of QML.

Practical Applications: Identifying and demonstrating practical applications of QML is crucial for its adoption. Fields such as drug discovery, materials science, finance, and cryptography are actively exploring the potential of QML to solve real-world problems.

Quantum algorithms for machine learning represent a promising frontier in computational science. By leveraging the principles of quantum mechanics, these algorithms have the potential to revolutionize the way we process data, optimize solutions, and recognize patterns. This chapter provides an in-depth exploration of key quantum algorithms for machine learning, including their concepts, mathematical frameworks, advantages, and applications. Understanding these algorithms is essential for harnessing the power of quantum computing in the field of machine learning.

This detailed chapter provides an in-depth exploration of quantum algorithms for machine learning, offering insights into their concepts, mathematical frameworks, advantages, and applications. This knowledge is essential for effectively integrating quantum computing with machine learning and advancing the field of quantum machine learning.

Chapter 8:

Quantum Neural Networks (QNNs) and Quantum Computing

Introduction to Quantum Neural Networks (QNNs)

Definition and Overview: Quantum Neural Networks (QNNs) are quantum counterparts to classical neural networks. They leverage quantum computing's unique properties, such as superposition and entanglement, to enhance the capabilities of neural networks. QNNs aim to improve upon classical neural networks in terms of expressiveness, training efficiency, and computational power.

Motivation: The motivation behind QNNs arises from the limitations of classical neural networks in processing high-dimensional data, handling complex models, and achieving efficient training. Quantum neural networks offer the potential to overcome these limitations by utilizing quantum parallelism and leveraging the high-dimensional Hilbert space.

Components of Quantum Neural Networks

Quantum Gates and Qubits:

Quantum Gates: Quantum gates are the fundamental operations in quantum computing, analogous to classical logic gates. They perform unitary transformations on qubits, manipulating their states. Common quantum gates used in QNNs include Hadamard gates, Pauli gates, and rotation gates.

Qubits: Qubits are the basic units of quantum information. Unlike classical bits, qubits can exist in a superposition of states, allowing for more complex and powerful computations. The manipulation and measurement of qubits are central to quantum neural network operations.

Quantum Circuits: Quantum circuits consist of qubits and quantum gates arranged in a sequence to perform computations. In QNNs, quantum circuits are used to represent neural network layers, where each layer applies a series of quantum gates to the input quantum states.

Quantum Layers: Quantum layers are analogous to layers in classical neural networks. Each quantum layer applies a specific set of quantum gates to the qubits, transforming the input quantum state into an output state. Quantum layers can include operations such as rotations, entanglements, and measurements.

Training Quantum Neural Networks

Quantum Backpropagation:

Concept: Quantum backpropagation is a training algorithm used to optimize the parameters of a quantum neural network. It is analogous to classical backpropagation but adapted for quantum circuits. The goal is to minimize the loss function by adjusting the parameters of quantum gates.

Mathematical Framework: Quantum backpropagation involves computing the gradient of the loss function with respect to the quantum gate parameters. This requires evaluating the output of the quantum circuit and calculating the derivatives of the loss function. Techniques such as parameter shift rules and quantum gradient descent are used to perform these calculations efficiently.

Challenges:

Gradient Estimation: Estimating gradients in quantum circuits can be challenging due to the probabilistic nature of quantum measurements.

Parameter Optimization: Optimizing quantum gate parameters requires efficient algorithms to handle the high-dimensional parameter space.

Variational Quantum Algorithms:

Concept: Variational quantum algorithms use a parameterized quantum circuit to approximate solutions to optimization problems. The parameters are optimized using classical optimization techniques to minimize a cost function. Variational Quantum Eigensolver (VQE) and Quantum Approximate Optimization Algorithm (QAOA) are examples of variational algorithms used in QNNs.

Mathematical Framework: In variational quantum algorithms, the quantum circuit is parameterized by a set of variables. The cost function is computed by measuring the output of the quantum circuit, and classical optimization techniques are used to adjust the parameters. The goal is to find the optimal parameters that minimize the cost function.

Advantages:

Flexibility: Variational algorithms can be adapted to different types of quantum circuits and optimization problems.

Error Mitigation: Variational methods can mitigate the impact of quantum noise by optimizing over a limited number of parameters.

Applications:

Optimization Problems: Variational algorithms are used to solve combinatorial optimization problems, such as graph coloring and portfolio optimization.
Quantum Chemistry: Variational algorithms are used to compute molecular properties and simulate quantum systems.

Quantum Neural Network Architectures

Quantum Perceptron:

Concept: The quantum perceptron is the simplest form of a quantum neural network, analogous to a classical perceptron. It consists of a single quantum layer that performs a linear transformation on the input qubits followed by a measurement.

Mathematical Framework: The quantum perceptron applies a series of quantum gates to the input qubits, resulting in a quantum state that is then measured to produce an output. The parameters of the quantum gates are adjusted during training to minimize the error.

Applications:

Binary Classification: Quantum perceptrons can be used for binary classification tasks, such as image recognition and signal detection.

Quantum Feedforward Neural Networks:

Concept: Quantum feedforward neural networks consist of multiple quantum layers arranged in a sequence. Each layer applies quantum gates to transform the input quantum state, and the output is used as the input for the next layer.

Mathematical Framework: Quantum feedforward networks apply a series of unitary transformations to the input qubits. The network architecture can include multiple layers of quantum gates, with each layer performing specific operations. The output of the network is obtained by measuring the final quantum state.

Applications:

Pattern Recognition: Quantum feedforward networks can be used for pattern recognition tasks, such as image and speech processing.

Quantum Convolutional Neural Networks:

Concept: Quantum convolutional neural networks (QCNNs) extend classical convolutional neural networks (CNNs) to the quantum domain. QCNNs use quantum gates to perform convolution operations and pooling on quantum states.

Mathematical Framework: QCNNs apply quantum convolutional layers that perform local operations on subsets of qubits. The pooling operations are implemented using quantum gates that reduce the dimensionality of the quantum state. The network is trained using quantum backpropagation.

Applications:

Image Processing: QCNNs are used for image processing tasks, such as feature extraction and image classification.

Implementing Quantum Neural Networks

Quantum Hardware and Software:

Quantum Hardware: Quantum neural networks require quantum hardware capable of performing complex quantum computations. Current quantum hardware includes superconducting qubits, trapped ions, and photonic qubits. Each type of hardware has its own advantages and limitations.

Quantum Software: Quantum software platforms, such as IBM Qiskit, Google Cirq, and Microsoft Q#, provide tools for designing, simulating, and running quantum circuits. These platforms are used to implement and test quantum neural networks.

Challenges:

Hardware Constraints: Current quantum hardware has limited qubit count and gate fidelity, affecting the scalability and accuracy of QNNs.

Software Development: Developing efficient quantum algorithms and software tools is crucial for the practical implementation of QNNs.

Error Mitigation and Correction:

Error Mitigation: Error mitigation techniques are used to reduce the impact of quantum noise and errors on quantum computations. Techniques such as error-correcting codes, noise reduction algorithms, and circuit optimization are employed to improve the reliability of QNNs.

Error Correction: Quantum error correction involves encoding quantum information in a way that protects it from errors. Quantum error-correcting codes, such as the surface code and the Shor code, are used to detect and correct errors in quantum computations.

Future Directions in Quantum Neural Networks

Scalability and Practicality: Scaling QNNs to handle larger datasets and more complex models is a key area of research. Developing practical QNN architectures that can be implemented on current quantum hardware is essential for advancing the field.

Integration with Classical Methods: Combining QNNs with classical neural networks and hybrid quantum-classical approaches can enhance the capabilities of both systems. Hybrid methods leverage quantum computing for specific tasks while using classical methods for others.

Applications and Use Cases: Exploring new applications of QNNs in various domains, such as drug discovery, financial modeling, and materials science, is crucial for demonstrating their practical value. Identifying and addressing real-world problems that can benefit from QNNs will drive further research and development.

Quantum Neural Networks represent a transformative approach to neural network computation by leveraging the unique properties of quantum mechanics.

Understanding their components, training methods, architectures, and implementation challenges is essential for advancing the field of quantum machine learning. This chapter provides a comprehensive overview of QNNs, laying the groundwork for further exploration of quantum computing's potential in neural network applications.

This detailed chapter provides an in-depth exploration of Quantum Neural Networks, covering their components, training methods, architectures, implementation challenges, and future directions. This knowledge is crucial for harnessing the power of quantum computing in neural network applications and advancing the field of quantum machine learning.

Chapter 9: **Quantum-enhanced Optimization Techniques**

Introduction to Quantum-enhanced Optimization

Definition and Significance: Quantum-enhanced optimization refers to the application of quantum computing techniques to improve the efficiency and performance of optimization algorithms. Optimization is a fundamental task in machine learning and many other fields, involving the process of finding the best solution from a set of possible solutions. Quantum computing offers the potential to significantly accelerate and enhance optimization processes by leveraging quantum principles such as superposition, entanglement, and interference.

Motivation: Classical optimization techniques often face challenges related to computational complexity, especially for high-dimensional and combinatorial problems. Quantum-enhanced optimization aims to address these challenges by exploiting quantum algorithms that can provide speedups and improved performance for various optimization tasks.

Quantum Optimization Algorithms

Quantum Approximate Optimization Algorithm (QAOA):

Concept: The Quantum Approximate Optimization Algorithm (QAOA) is a variational quantum algorithm designed to solve combinatorial optimization problems. It is a hybrid quantum-classical algorithm that uses a quantum circuit to prepare a quantum state representing a superposition of potential solutions and a classical optimizer to adjust the parameters of the quantum circuit.

Mathematical Framework: QAOA involves the following steps:

Initialization: Prepare a uniform superposition of all possible solutions using a quantum circuit.

Quantum Circuit: Apply a sequence of unitary operations to encode the optimization problem into the quantum state.

Measurement: Measure the quantum state to obtain candidate solutions.

Optimization: Use classical optimization techniques to adjust the parameters of the quantum circuit to improve the solution.

Advantages:

Flexibility: QAOA can be applied to a wide range of combinatorial optimization problems.

Hybrid Nature: Combines quantum and classical techniques to leverage the strengths of both.

Applications:

Graph Problems: Vertex cover, traveling salesman problem, and max-cut problem.
Scheduling: Job scheduling and resource allocation.

Quantum Annealing:

Concept: Quantum annealing is a quantum optimization technique used to find the minimum of a cost function over a set of possible solutions. It is based on the principles of quantum mechanics, specifically quantum tunneling, which allows the system to escape local minima and find the global minimum more efficiently.

Mathematical Framework: Quantum annealing involves the following steps:

Initialization: Prepare the system in a known quantum state.
Annealing Process: Evolve the system according to a time-dependent Hamiltonian that represents the optimization problem.
Measurement: Measure the final quantum state to obtain the solution.

Advantages:

Global Minima: Quantum annealing can help escape local minima and find global optima.
Efficiency: Potentially more efficient for large and complex optimization problems.

Applications:

Combinatorial Optimization: Max-cut, graph partitioning, and integer programming.
Machine Learning: Hyperparameter tuning and feature selection.

Variational Quantum Eigensolver (VQE):

Concept: The Variational Quantum Eigensolver (VQE) is a variational quantum algorithm used to find the lowest eigenvalue of a Hamiltonian, which corresponds to the optimal solution of an optimization problem. VQE is particularly useful for problems where the Hamiltonian can be expressed in terms of a quantum circuit.

Mathematical Framework: VQE involves the following steps:

Quantum Circuit: Prepare a parameterized quantum circuit that represents the Hamiltonian.

Measurement: Measure the quantum state to obtain the energy of the Hamiltonian.

Optimization: Use classical optimization techniques to adjust the parameters of the quantum circuit to minimize the energy.

Advantages:

Flexibility: Can be applied to various types of Hamiltonians and optimization problems.

Error Mitigation: Variational methods can help mitigate the impact of quantum noise.

Applications:

Quantum Chemistry: Calculating molecular energies and properties.

Material Science: Modeling and optimizing material properties.

Quantum Subspace Expansion (QSE):

Concept: Quantum Subspace Expansion (QSE) is a technique used to enhance optimization algorithms by expanding the solution space using quantum superposition. It involves preparing a quantum state that represents a subspace of potential solutions and using quantum operations to explore this subspace.

Mathematical Framework: QSE involves the following steps:

Subspace Preparation: Prepare a quantum state that represents a subspace of potential solutions.
Quantum Operations: Apply quantum operations to explore and refine the subspace.
Measurement: Measure the quantum state to obtain candidate solutions.

Advantages:

Enhanced Exploration: Expands the solution space to explore a broader range of potential solutions.
Improved Accuracy: Can lead to more accurate and reliable solutions.

Applications:

Complex Optimization Problems: Problems with large and complex solution spaces.
Machine Learning: Enhancing optimization in training and hyperparameter tuning.

Implementing Quantum-enhanced Optimization Techniques

Quantum Hardware Requirements: Implementing quantum-enhanced optimization techniques requires quantum hardware capable of performing complex quantum computations. Current quantum hardware, such as superconducting qubits and trapped ions, provides the necessary capabilities for these algorithms.

Quantum Software and Tools: Quantum software platforms, such as IBM Qiskit, Google Cirq, and Microsoft Q#, offer tools for designing, simulating, and running quantum circuits. These platforms provide the infrastructure for implementing and testing quantum-enhanced optimization algorithms.

Hybrid Quantum-Classical Approaches: Many quantum-enhanced optimization techniques involve a hybrid approach, combining quantum and classical methods. Hybrid algorithms leverage quantum computing for specific tasks while using classical optimization techniques to handle others. Examples include QAOA and VQE.

Challenges and Future Directions

Hardware Limitations: Current quantum hardware has limitations in terms of qubit count, gate fidelity, and error rates. Developing robust quantum-enhanced optimization algorithms that can perform well on Noisy Intermediate-Scale Quantum (NISQ) devices is a key challenge.

Algorithmic Complexity: Designing efficient quantum-enhanced optimization algorithms involves overcoming the complexity of quantum state preparation, quantum operations, and measurement. Ongoing research is focused on developing algorithms that balance efficiency and resource requirements.

Scalability: Scaling quantum-enhanced optimization techniques to handle large datasets and complex problems remains a challenge. Researchers are exploring methods to improve the scalability and practical applicability of these techniques.

Practical Applications: Identifying and demonstrating practical applications of quantum-enhanced optimization is crucial for its adoption. Fields such as finance, logistics, and machine learning are actively exploring the potential of these techniques to solve real-world problems.

Quantum-enhanced optimization techniques represent a promising advancement in computational optimization by leveraging the principles of quantum computing. This chapter provides a comprehensive overview of key quantum optimization algorithms, including QAOA, quantum annealing, VQE, and QSE. Understanding these techniques and their implementation challenges is essential for harnessing the power of quantum computing in optimization tasks. As quantum technology continues to advance, these techniques will play a critical role in solving complex and high-dimensional optimization problems.

This detailed chapter explores quantum-enhanced optimization techniques, covering key algorithms, their mathematical frameworks, advantages, applications, and implementation challenges. This knowledge is crucial for advancing the field of quantum optimization and integrating quantum computing with optimization tasks.

Chapter 10:

Quantum Machine Learning in Practice

Introduction to Quantum Machine Learning in Practice

Definition and Importance: Quantum Machine Learning (QML) refers to the integration of quantum computing techniques with machine learning algorithms to enhance computational capabilities. In practice, QML aims to solve real-world problems more efficiently than classical methods by leveraging quantum principles such as superposition and entanglement. The practical application of QML involves developing and implementing algorithms that can provide tangible benefits in various domains.

Motivation: The motivation for applying QML in practice stems from the limitations of classical machine learning techniques, especially when dealing with large datasets and complex models. Quantum computing offers potential advantages in terms of speed, accuracy, and efficiency. The goal is to translate theoretical advances in QML into practical solutions that can address real-world challenges.

Key Areas of Practical Application

Quantum-enhanced Data Processing:

Concept: Quantum-enhanced data processing involves using quantum algorithms to accelerate data processing tasks such as data cleaning, feature extraction, and dimensionality reduction. These tasks are crucial for preparing data for machine learning algorithms.

Applications:

Data Cleaning: Quantum algorithms can potentially speed up the process of identifying and correcting errors in large datasets.

Feature Extraction: Quantum techniques can enhance feature extraction by exploring high-dimensional feature spaces more efficiently.

Dimensionality Reduction: Quantum algorithms, such as Quantum Principal Component Analysis (QPCA), can reduce the dimensionality of data while preserving essential features.

Challenges:

Data Representation: Efficiently representing classical data in quantum states.

Error Handling: Managing errors and noise in quantum data processing.

Quantum-enhanced Classification:

Concept: Quantum-enhanced classification involves applying quantum algorithms to improve the performance of classification tasks. Quantum classifiers leverage quantum superposition and entanglement to make predictions based on quantum-encoded data.

Applications:

Quantum Support Vector Machines (QSVMs): QSVMs use quantum algorithms to classify data in high-dimensional feature spaces.
Quantum Neural Networks (QNNs): QNNs can be used for complex classification tasks by utilizing quantum circuits to process data.

Challenges:

Scalability: Ensuring that quantum classifiers can handle large-scale datasets.
Interpretability: Understanding and interpreting the results produced by quantum classifiers.

Quantum-enhanced Clustering:

Concept: Quantum-enhanced clustering involves using quantum algorithms to group data into clusters based on similarity. Quantum clustering algorithms aim to improve the accuracy and efficiency of clustering tasks.

Applications:

Quantum k-means Clustering: Quantum k-means can enhance clustering performance by exploring multiple cluster assignments simultaneously.
Quantum Clustering Algorithms: Various quantum algorithms can be used to partition data into meaningful clusters.

Challenges:

Algorithm Complexity: Developing efficient quantum clustering algorithms.
Data Preparation: Preparing data for quantum clustering algorithms.

Quantum-enhanced Optimization for Machine Learning:

Concept: Quantum-enhanced optimization techniques can be used to improve the performance of machine learning algorithms by optimizing hyperparameters, feature selection, and model training.

Applications:

Hyperparameter Tuning: Quantum algorithms can optimize hyperparameters to enhance model performance.

Feature Selection: Quantum-enhanced optimization can identify relevant features for machine learning models.

Model Training: Quantum algorithms can accelerate the training process of machine learning models.

Challenges:

Resource Requirements: Ensuring that quantum-enhanced optimization techniques can be implemented with available quantum hardware.

Integration: Integrating quantum optimization with classical machine learning workflows.

Implementing QML Algorithms

Quantum Hardware and Software Platforms:

Quantum Hardware: Implementing QML algorithms requires access to quantum hardware capable of performing complex quantum computations. Current quantum hardware includes superconducting qubits, trapped ions, and photonic qubits, each with its own advantages and limitations.

Quantum Software: Quantum software platforms, such as IBM Qiskit, Google Cirq, and Microsoft Q#, provide tools for designing, simulating, and running quantum circuits. These platforms are essential for developing and testing QML algorithms.

Hybrid Quantum-Classical Approaches: Many practical QML applications involve hybrid quantum-classical approaches, where quantum algorithms are used for specific tasks, and classical methods handle other aspects. Examples include Variational Quantum Eigensolver (VQE) and Quantum Approximate Optimization Algorithm (QAOA).

Case Studies of QML in Practice

Case Study 1: Drug Discovery

Overview: QML has the potential to revolutionize drug discovery by accelerating the process of identifying and optimizing drug candidates. Quantum algorithms can simulate molecular interactions and explore chemical spaces more efficiently than classical methods.

Application:

Molecular Simulations: Quantum simulations can provide accurate predictions of molecular properties and interactions.

Optimization: Quantum-enhanced optimization techniques can identify promising drug candidates by exploring large chemical spaces.

Challenges:

Hardware Limitations: Access to quantum hardware with sufficient qubits and accuracy.
Integration with Classical Methods: Combining quantum simulations with classical data and models.

Case Study 2: Financial Modeling

Overview: QML can be applied to financial modeling tasks such as risk analysis, portfolio optimization, and fraud detection. Quantum algorithms can improve the accuracy and efficiency of financial models by leveraging quantum computational power.

Application:

Portfolio Optimization: Quantum algorithms can optimize investment portfolios by exploring large solution spaces.
Risk Analysis: Quantum-enhanced models can provide more accurate risk assessments.

Challenges:

Data Privacy: Ensuring the security and privacy of financial data in quantum computations.

Algorithm Development: Developing algorithms that can be effectively implemented on current quantum hardware.

Case Study 3: Image and Speech Recognition

Overview: QML can enhance image and speech recognition tasks by improving the accuracy and efficiency of recognition algorithms. Quantum-enhanced neural networks and classifiers can process high-dimensional data more effectively.

Application:

Image Recognition: Quantum Neural Networks (QNNs) can be used for image classification and object detection.
Speech Recognition: Quantum algorithms can improve speech recognition accuracy by processing complex audio signals.

Challenges:

Data Preparation: Preparing high-dimensional data for quantum algorithms.
Model Training: Training quantum-enhanced models with current hardware constraints.

Future Directions and Research Opportunities

Scaling Quantum Algorithms: Scaling QML algorithms to handle larger datasets and more complex models is a key area of research. Advances in quantum hardware and software will play a crucial role in addressing these challenges.

Integration with Classical Systems: Developing methods to integrate QML algorithms with classical systems and workflows is essential for practical applications. Hybrid approaches that combine quantum and classical techniques will be important for real-world implementations.

Exploring New Applications: Identifying and exploring new applications of QML in various fields, such as healthcare, finance, and artificial intelligence, will drive further research and development. Practical use cases will demonstrate the value of QML in solving real-world problems.

Quantum Machine Learning represents a transformative approach to solving complex problems by leveraging quantum computing principles. This chapter provides a comprehensive overview of practical applications, including data processing, classification, clustering, and optimization. Understanding the implementation of QML algorithms and exploring real-world case studies are crucial for advancing the field and translating theoretical advances into practical solutions. As quantum technology continues to evolve, QML will play an increasingly important role in addressing real-world challenges and advancing computational capabilities.

This detailed chapter explores the practical application of Quantum Machine Learning, covering key areas such as data processing, classification, clustering, and optimization. It also includes case studies and future research directions, providing a comprehensive understanding of how QML can be effectively applied to solve real-world problems.

Chapter 11:

Quantum Computing for Natural Language Processing (NLP)

Introduction to Quantum Computing for NLP

Definition and Relevance: Quantum Computing for Natural Language Processing (NLP) involves applying quantum computing techniques to improve and innovate NLP tasks. NLP, a field at the intersection of artificial intelligence and linguistics, focuses on enabling machines to understand, interpret, and generate human language. Quantum computing offers potential advantages in NLP by leveraging quantum superposition, entanglement, and quantum parallelism to enhance performance and efficiency.

Motivation: The increasing complexity of NLP tasks and the limitations of classical computing in handling large-scale language models motivate the exploration of quantum computing for NLP. Quantum algorithms could potentially accelerate training times, improve model accuracy, and enable new capabilities in language understanding and generation.

Quantum Algorithms for NLP

Quantum-enhanced Language Models:

Concept: Quantum-enhanced language models aim to leverage quantum computing to improve the performance of models that process and generate natural language. These models use quantum algorithms to represent and manipulate language data more efficiently.

Quantum Neural Networks (QNNs): QNNs can be adapted for language modeling by encoding linguistic data into quantum states and using quantum circuits to process and generate language. The potential benefits include faster training times and enhanced model expressiveness.

Applications:

Text Generation: Quantum-enhanced models can generate coherent and contextually relevant text. **Language Understanding:** Improved comprehension of semantic and syntactic structures.

Challenges:

Data Encoding: Efficiently encoding text data into quantum states.

Model Training: Adapting quantum neural networks for language tasks.

Quantum Transformers:

Concept: Quantum Transformers are an adaptation of classical transformer models, which are widely used in NLP tasks such as translation and summarization. Quantum Transformers utilize quantum circuits to perform attention mechanisms and other operations more efficiently.

Mathematical Framework: Quantum Transformers involve replacing classical operations with quantum counterparts, such as quantum attention mechanisms and quantum feedforward layers. These modifications aim to leverage quantum parallelism and entanglement to enhance performance.

Applications:

Machine Translation: Quantum Transformers can improve translation accuracy and speed.
Text Summarization: Enhanced ability to generate concise and informative summaries.

Challenges:

Circuit Complexity: Designing quantum circuits that can perform transformer operations efficiently.

Scalability: Ensuring that quantum Transformers can handle large-scale NLP tasks.

Quantum-enhanced Information Retrieval:

Concept: Quantum-enhanced information retrieval involves using quantum computing to improve search and retrieval of information from large text corpora. Quantum algorithms can enhance the efficiency of searching for relevant documents and information.

Applications:

Search Engines: Quantum algorithms can optimize search queries and improve retrieval relevance.
Document Classification: Enhanced ability to classify and categorize documents.

Challenges:

Data Storage: Efficiently storing and accessing large text corpora in quantum systems.
Query Processing: Developing quantum algorithms for fast and accurate query processing.

Quantum-enhanced Sentiment Analysis:

Concept: Quantum-enhanced sentiment analysis uses quantum computing techniques to analyze and interpret the sentiment expressed in text. Quantum algorithms can potentially improve the accuracy and speed of sentiment classification.

Applications:

Opinion Mining: Enhanced ability to analyze and classify opinions and sentiments in text.
Customer Feedback: Improved analysis of customer reviews and feedback.

Challenges:

Text Representation: Representing textual sentiment data in quantum states.
Algorithm Development: Developing quantum algorithms for effective sentiment analysis.

Implementing Quantum NLP Algorithms

Quantum Hardware and Software Requirements:

Quantum Hardware: Implementing quantum NLP algorithms requires access to quantum hardware capable of performing complex quantum computations. Current hardware options include superconducting qubits, trapped ions, and photonic qubits, each with its own advantages and constraints.

Quantum Software: Quantum software platforms, such as IBM Qiskit, Google Cirq, and Microsoft Q#, provide tools for designing and simulating quantum circuits. These platforms are essential for developing and testing quantum NLP algorithms.

Data Preparation: Preparing text data for quantum NLP algorithms involves encoding linguistic data into quantum states. Techniques such as quantum embeddings and quantum state preparation are used to represent text data in a format suitable for quantum processing.

Case Studies in Quantum NLP

Case Study 1: Quantum-enhanced Text Generation

Overview: Quantum-enhanced text generation explores using quantum algorithms to generate human-like text based on given prompts. Quantum language models can potentially offer improved coherence and context relevance compared to classical models.

Application:

Creative Writing: Generating stories, poems, and other creative text forms.
Content Creation: Enhancing content generation for marketing and media.

Challenges:

Model Complexity: Designing quantum models that generate high-quality text.

Training Data: Obtaining and preparing large datasets for training.

Case Study 2: Quantum-enhanced Machine Translation

Overview: Quantum-enhanced machine translation focuses on using quantum algorithms to improve translation accuracy and efficiency. Quantum Transformers can potentially offer better performance in translating between languages.

Application:

Cross-lingual Communication: Improving translation services for international communication.

Localization: Enhancing translation accuracy for software and content localization.

Challenges:

Language Representation: Encoding and processing multiple languages in quantum systems.

Computational Resources: Managing the computational resources required for large-scale translation tasks.

Case Study 3: Quantum-enhanced Sentiment Analysis

Overview: Quantum-enhanced sentiment analysis involves using quantum algorithms to analyze and classify sentiment in text data. Quantum techniques can potentially offer more accurate sentiment classification and faster processing times.

Application:

Social Media Analysis: Analyzing user sentiments on social media platforms.
Market Research: Improving sentiment analysis for market and consumer research.

Challenges:

Data Privacy: Ensuring the privacy and security of sentiment analysis data.
Algorithm Accuracy: Developing algorithms that accurately classify sentiment.

Future Directions and Research Opportunities

Scalability and Practicality: Scaling quantum NLP algorithms to handle large and diverse datasets is a key research area. Advancements in quantum hardware and software will be crucial for practical implementations.

Integration with Classical Systems: Developing hybrid quantum-classical approaches for NLP tasks can leverage the strengths of both quantum and classical methods. Hybrid models that combine quantum and classical techniques will be important for real-world applications.

Exploring New NLP Tasks: Identifying and exploring new NLP tasks that can benefit from quantum computing is essential for advancing the field. Emerging applications and use cases will drive further research and development.

Quantum Computing for Natural Language Processing offers exciting possibilities for enhancing and innovating NLP tasks. This chapter provides a comprehensive overview of quantum algorithms for NLP, including language models, transformers, information retrieval, and sentiment analysis. Understanding the implementation of quantum NLP algorithms and exploring real-world case studies are crucial for advancing the field and translating theoretical advances into practical solutions. As quantum technology continues to evolve, it will play an increasingly important role in revolutionizing how machines process and understand human language.

This detailed chapter explores the application of Quantum Computing to Natural Language Processing, covering key algorithms, case studies, and future research directions. It provides a comprehensive understanding of how quantum techniques can enhance and innovate various NLP tasks.

Chapter 12:

Quantum Computing for Data Privacy and Security

Introduction to Quantum Computing for Data Privacy and Security

Definition and Significance: Quantum computing for data privacy and security involves applying quantum computing principles and algorithms to enhance data protection mechanisms. Data privacy and security are critical concerns in the digital age, as traditional cryptographic methods face challenges from emerging quantum technologies. Quantum computing offers new approaches to both protecting data and understanding potential vulnerabilities introduced by quantum threats.

Motivation: The advent of quantum computing introduces both opportunities and risks for data security. While quantum algorithms can provide novel methods for securing data, they also pose threats to existing cryptographic protocols. Addressing these challenges is essential for ensuring the integrity and confidentiality of sensitive information in a quantum-enabled world.

Quantum Cryptography

Quantum Key Distribution (QKD):

Concept: Quantum Key Distribution (QKD) is a quantum cryptographic technique that allows two parties to securely share a secret key using quantum mechanics principles. QKD leverages the principles of quantum superposition and entanglement to ensure that any eavesdropping attempts are detectable.

Mathematical Framework: QKD protocols involve:

Quantum State Preparation: Preparing and transmitting quantum states (e.g., photons) between parties.
Measurement: Measuring the quantum states to extract key information.
Key Reconciliation: Comparing and correcting the shared key to ensure its security.

Advantages:

Unconditional Security: The security of QKD is based on the laws of quantum mechanics rather than computational assumptions.
Eavesdropping Detection: Any eavesdropping attempts can be detected through changes in the quantum states.

Applications:

Secure Communication: Ensuring the confidentiality of messages transmitted over insecure channels.
Key Management: Safely distributing encryption keys for secure communications.

Challenges:

Infrastructure Requirements: Implementing QKD requires specialized hardware and infrastructure.
Distance Limitations: Quantum signals can be attenuated over long distances, limiting QKD effectiveness.

Post-Quantum Cryptography:

Concept: Post-Quantum Cryptography (PQC) refers to cryptographic algorithms designed to be secure against attacks from quantum computers. PQC aims to develop algorithms that remain secure even in the presence of powerful quantum adversaries.

Mathematical Framework: PQC involves:

Algorithm Design: Creating cryptographic algorithms that are resistant to quantum attacks.
Security Analysis: Evaluating the security of algorithms against quantum and classical threats.

Advantages:

Future-Proofing: Ensures that cryptographic methods remain secure as quantum computing technology advances.
Wide Applicability: Can be applied to various cryptographic tasks, including encryption and digital signatures.

Applications:

Public Key Infrastructure (PKI): Securing digital communications and transactions.
Data Encryption: Protecting sensitive data from quantum-enabled decryption.

Challenges:

Performance Trade-offs: Balancing security with algorithm efficiency and practicality.
Standardization: Developing and standardizing PQC algorithms for widespread adoption.

Quantum Attacks and Countermeasures

Quantum Algorithms for Breaking Classical Cryptography:

Concept: Quantum algorithms, such as Shor's algorithm and Grover's algorithm, pose potential threats to classical cryptographic protocols. Shor's algorithm can efficiently factorize large integers, threatening RSA encryption, while Grover's algorithm can accelerate brute-force attacks on symmetric ciphers.

Mathematical Framework:

Shor's Algorithm: Utilizes quantum Fourier transform to factorize integers in polynomial time.
Grover's Algorithm: Provides quadratic speedup for searching through unsorted databases.

Countermeasures:

Algorithmic Changes: Transitioning to post-quantum cryptographic algorithms to withstand quantum attacks.
Hybrid Approaches: Combining classical and quantum-resistant methods for added security.

Quantum Safe Encryption Techniques:

Concept: Quantum safe encryption techniques are designed to resist attacks from quantum computers. These techniques include lattice-based cryptography, code-based cryptography, and multivariate polynomial cryptography.

Mathematical Framework:

Lattice-Based Cryptography: Relies on the hardness of lattice problems, which are believed to be resistant to quantum attacks.

Code-Based Cryptography: Based on the difficulty of decoding random linear codes.

Multivariate Polynomial Cryptography: Involves solving systems of multivariate polynomial equations, a problem resistant to quantum algorithms.

Applications:

Secure Communications: Protecting data against quantum-enabled decryption attempts.

Digital Signatures: Ensuring the authenticity and integrity of digital documents.

Challenges:

Algorithm Efficiency: Ensuring that quantum-safe encryption methods are efficient and practical.

Integration: Incorporating quantum-safe techniques into existing cryptographic systems.

Implementing Quantum Data Privacy Solutions

Quantum Hardware and Software Requirements:

Quantum Hardware: Implementing quantum cryptographic solutions requires access to quantum hardware capable of performing quantum computations and communication. Technologies such as superconducting qubits and photonic qubits are used for quantum key distribution and other cryptographic tasks.

Quantum Software: Quantum software platforms, such as IBM Qiskit and Google Cirq, provide tools for developing and testing quantum cryptographic algorithms. These platforms enable researchers to simulate and implement quantum cryptographic protocols.

Data Preparation and Management:

Quantum Data Encoding: Representing classical data in quantum states for secure processing.
Key Management Systems: Developing systems to manage and distribute quantum-generated keys securely.

Case Studies in Quantum Data Privacy

Case Study 1: Secure Communication with QKD

Overview: Quantum Key Distribution (QKD) has been successfully implemented in various secure communication systems. Real-world deployments demonstrate the practical benefits of QKD for secure key exchange and communication.

Application:

Financial Sector: Using QKD to secure financial transactions and communications.
Government Communications: Ensuring the confidentiality of sensitive government communications.

Challenges:

Infrastructure Costs: High costs associated with deploying and maintaining QKD infrastructure.
Distance Limitations: Addressing the challenges of transmitting quantum signals over long distances.

Case Study 2: Post-Quantum Cryptographic Algorithms in Practice

Overview: Post-Quantum Cryptographic (PQC) algorithms are being evaluated and standardized for practical use. Case studies highlight the transition to PQC methods and their integration into existing cryptographic systems.

Application:

Public Key Encryption: Implementing PQC algorithms for secure public key encryption.
Digital Signatures: Transitioning to PQC algorithms for secure digital signatures.

Challenges:

Algorithm Performance: Balancing the performance of PQC algorithms with security requirements.
Standardization: Ensuring broad adoption and standardization of PQC algorithms.

Future Directions and Research Opportunities

Advancing Quantum Hardware: Continued development of quantum hardware is crucial for implementing practical quantum cryptographic solutions. Improving qubit fidelity, increasing qubit count, and enhancing quantum communication technologies are key areas of focus.

Developing Hybrid Solutions: Hybrid quantum-classical approaches that combine quantum cryptographic methods with classical techniques will be important for practical implementations. Research into hybrid solutions can provide added security and functionality.

Exploring New Cryptographic Protocols: Researching and developing new quantum cryptographic protocols and algorithms will drive innovation in data privacy and security. Exploring novel approaches to secure data in a quantum-enabled world is essential for advancing the field.

Quantum Computing for Data Privacy and Security offers transformative possibilities for enhancing data protection mechanisms and addressing emerging threats. This chapter provides a comprehensive overview of quantum cryptography, including Quantum Key Distribution, Post-Quantum Cryptography, and quantum attacks and countermeasures. Understanding the implementation of quantum data privacy solutions and exploring real-world case studies are crucial for advancing the field and ensuring robust security in a quantum-enabled world. As quantum technology continues to evolve, it will play a pivotal role in shaping the future of data privacy and security.

This detailed chapter explores the application of Quantum Computing to Data Privacy and Security, covering key concepts, algorithms, case studies, and future research directions. It provides a thorough understanding of how quantum techniques can enhance and innovate data protection methods and address potential vulnerabilities introduced by quantum technologies.

Chapter 13:

Quantum Computing for Optimization Problems

Introduction to Quantum Computing for Optimization Problems

Definition and Importance: Optimization problems involve finding the best solution from a set of possible solutions under given constraints. These problems are prevalent in various fields, including logistics, finance, engineering, and machine learning. Quantum computing offers novel approaches to solving optimization problems by leveraging quantum principles to explore solution spaces more efficiently than classical methods.

Motivation: Traditional optimization techniques often struggle with large, complex problems due to exponential growth in the number of possible solutions. Quantum computing provides the potential to significantly speed up the process of finding optimal solutions by utilizing quantum parallelism and superposition. This chapter explores how quantum computing can address optimization challenges and improve problem-solving efficiency.

Quantum Optimization Algorithms

Quantum Approximate Optimization Algorithm (QAOA):

Concept: The Quantum Approximate Optimization Algorithm (QAOA) is a quantum algorithm designed to find approximate solutions to combinatorial optimization problems. QAOA utilizes quantum circuits to explore different solutions and optimize objective functions.

Mathematical Framework: QAOA involves:

Problem Encoding: Encoding the optimization problem into a quantum circuit.
Parameterized Quantum Circuits: Using parameterized quantum gates to create superpositions of possible solutions.
Cost Function Evaluation: Measuring the quantum state to evaluate the cost function and iteratively adjust parameters to minimize the cost.

Advantages:

Flexibility: QAOA can be applied to various combinatorial optimization problems.
Approximation: Provides approximate solutions with a trade-off between solution quality and computational resources.

Applications:

Scheduling: Optimizing scheduling tasks for manufacturing and resource allocation.
Traveling Salesman Problem: Finding near-optimal routes for salesmen visiting multiple cities.

Challenges:

Circuit Depth: Managing the depth and complexity of quantum circuits.
Parameter Tuning: Efficiently tuning parameters to improve solution quality.

Variational Quantum Eigensolver (VQE):

Concept: The Variational Quantum Eigensolver (VQE) is a quantum algorithm used for finding the lowest eigenvalue of a Hamiltonian, which can be applied to optimization problems. VQE combines quantum and classical methods to optimize objective functions.

Mathematical Framework: VQE involves:

Hamiltonian Representation: Representing the optimization problem as a Hamiltonian operator.
Quantum State Preparation: Using a quantum circuit to prepare states that approximate the ground state of the Hamiltonian.

Classical Optimization: Utilizing classical optimization algorithms to adjust quantum circuit parameters and minimize the energy expectation value.

Advantages:

Quantum-Classical Hybrid: Combines quantum computation with classical optimization techniques.
Scalability: Can handle large-scale optimization problems with moderate quantum resources.

Applications:

Quantum Chemistry: Optimizing molecular structures and energies.
Machine Learning: Enhancing training and optimization of quantum machine learning models.

Challenges:

Noise and Decoherence: Managing errors and noise in quantum computations.
Convergence: Ensuring convergence to the global minimum of the cost function.

Quantum Annealing:

Concept: Quantum Annealing is a quantum optimization technique that leverages quantum tunneling to find the global minimum of a cost function. Quantum annealers use a quantum mechanical process to escape local minima and converge to optimal solutions.

Mathematical Framework: Quantum Annealing involves:

Problem Mapping: Encoding the optimization problem into an Ising or Quadratic Unconstrained Binary Optimization (QUBO) model.

Annealing Process: Evolving the system from a superposition of states to a low-energy state using quantum annealing techniques.

Solution Extraction: Measuring the final quantum state to obtain the optimal or near-optimal solution.

Advantages:

Escaping Local Minima: Quantum annealing can escape local minima that trap classical optimization methods.

Global Optimization: Provides a potential pathway to finding the global minimum.

Applications:

Financial Optimization: Portfolio optimization and risk management.

Logistics: Optimizing supply chain and transportation networks.

Challenges:

Hardware Limitations: The effectiveness of quantum annealers depends on the available quantum hardware. **Problem Encoding:** Efficiently encoding real-world problems into quantum annealing models.

Implementing Quantum Optimization Algorithms

Quantum Hardware and Software Requirements:

Quantum Hardware: Implementing quantum optimization algorithms requires access to quantum hardware that can perform complex quantum computations. Quantum processors used for optimization include superconducting qubits and quantum annealers, each with its own capabilities and constraints.

Quantum Software: Quantum software platforms, such as IBM Qiskit, D-Wave Ocean, and Google Cirq, provide tools for developing and testing quantum optimization algorithms. These platforms facilitate the design, simulation, and execution of quantum optimization tasks.

Algorithm Development: Developing quantum optimization algorithms involves:

Algorithm Design: Designing quantum algorithms tailored to specific optimization problems.

Performance Evaluation: Testing and evaluating the performance of quantum algorithms against classical methods.

Case Studies in Quantum Optimization

Case Study 1: Optimization in Logistics

Overview: Quantum optimization has been applied to logistics and supply chain management, where complex optimization problems arise. Quantum algorithms offer potential improvements in route planning, inventory management, and distribution strategies.

Application:

Route Optimization: Using quantum algorithms to find optimal routes for transportation and delivery.

Inventory Management: Enhancing inventory control and demand forecasting.

Challenges:

Data Integration: Integrating quantum optimization with existing logistics systems.

Scalability: Addressing the scalability of quantum algorithms for large logistics networks.

Case Study 2: Financial Portfolio Optimization

Overview: Quantum optimization techniques are being explored for financial portfolio optimization, where the goal is to allocate assets to maximize returns and minimize risk. Quantum algorithms provide potential advantages in handling complex financial models.

Application:

Risk Management: Using quantum algorithms to optimize risk and return trade-offs in investment portfolios.

Asset Allocation: Enhancing portfolio performance through quantum-enhanced optimization.

Challenges:

Data Privacy: Ensuring the privacy and security of financial data during optimization.

Algorithm Efficiency: Balancing the efficiency of quantum algorithms with real-world financial constraints.

Case Study 3: Quantum Chemistry Optimization

Overview: Quantum optimization has significant applications in quantum chemistry, where it is used to optimize molecular structures and energies. Quantum algorithms provide potential improvements in computational chemistry simulations.

Application:

Molecular Design: Using quantum algorithms to optimize molecular structures for drug discovery and materials science.

Energy Minimization: Enhancing the accuracy of energy calculations for chemical reactions.

Challenges:

Hardware Requirements: Meeting the computational demands of quantum chemistry simulations.

Algorithm Development: Developing algorithms that can effectively model chemical systems.

Future Directions and Research Opportunities

Advancing Quantum Hardware: Continued development of quantum hardware is crucial for implementing practical quantum optimization solutions. Improvements in qubit quality, connectivity, and coherence are essential for solving complex optimization problems.

Hybrid Quantum-Classical Approaches:
Developing hybrid quantum-classical approaches that combine quantum optimization with classical methods

can leverage the strengths of both technologies. Hybrid models will be important for practical applications in various fields.

Exploring New Optimization Problems:
Identifying and exploring new optimization problems that can benefit from quantum computing will drive further research and development. Emerging applications and use cases will advance the field of quantum optimization.

Quantum Computing for Optimization Problems offers transformative possibilities for solving complex optimization challenges more efficiently than classical methods. This chapter provides a comprehensive overview of quantum optimization algorithms, including QAOA, VQE, and Quantum Annealing, and explores real-world case studies demonstrating their potential benefits. Understanding the implementation of quantum optimization algorithms and exploring future research opportunities are crucial for advancing the field and translating theoretical advances into practical solutions. As quantum technology continues to evolve, it will play a pivotal role in addressing optimization problems across various domains.

This detailed chapter explores the application of Quantum Computing to Optimization Problems, covering key algorithms, case studies, and future research directions. It provides a thorough understanding of how quantum techniques can enhance and innovate solutions to complex optimization challenges.

Chapter 14:

Future Trends and Challenges in Quantum Machine Learning

Introduction to Future Trends and Challenges

Definition and Significance: As quantum machine learning (QML) continues to evolve, it promises to revolutionize the field of machine learning by leveraging quantum computing's unique capabilities. Future trends in QML will shape how quantum algorithms are developed, implemented, and integrated into practical applications. Understanding the potential challenges and opportunities that lie ahead is crucial for advancing the field and realizing the benefits of QML.

Motivation: The rapid advancement of quantum computing technology and its potential impact on machine learning presents both exciting opportunities and significant challenges. Identifying and addressing these trends and challenges will be essential for driving innovation and achieving practical breakthroughs in QML.

Future Trends in Quantum Machine Learning

Development of New Quantum Algorithms:

Concept: The development of new quantum algorithms tailored to machine learning tasks will be a major trend in QML. These algorithms will aim to leverage quantum computing's strengths, such as superposition and entanglement, to improve performance and efficiency.

Trends:

Quantum Kernels: Development of quantum kernel methods to enhance support vector machines and other kernel-based algorithms.
Quantum Neural Networks (QNNs):
Advancements in QNN architectures and training methods to improve their applicability to various machine learning tasks.
Hybrid Algorithms: Combining quantum and classical techniques to create hybrid algorithms that benefit from both quantum speedup and classical robustness.

Applications:

Pattern Recognition: Improving pattern recognition tasks such as image and speech recognition.

Data Classification: Enhancing classification algorithms for complex and high-dimensional data.

Challenges:

Algorithm Complexity: Designing quantum algorithms that are both effective and feasible with current hardware.
Benchmarking: Developing benchmarks to evaluate the performance of new quantum algorithms.

Advances in Quantum Hardware:

Concept: Advancements in quantum hardware will significantly impact the development and implementation of QML algorithms. Improvements in qubit technology, error correction, and quantum connectivity will enhance the capabilities of quantum computers for machine learning tasks.

Trends:

Increased Qubit Counts: Expanding the number of qubits to handle more complex computations and larger datasets.
Error Correction: Implementing advanced quantum error correction techniques to improve the reliability of quantum computations.

Quantum Hardware Integration: Integrating quantum processors with classical systems to facilitate hybrid quantum-classical approaches.

Applications:

Large-Scale Machine Learning: Enabling the processing of larger datasets and more complex models.
Real-Time Computation: Improving the speed and efficiency of real-time machine learning applications.

Challenges:

Scalability: Scaling up quantum hardware to handle practical machine learning tasks.
Error Rates: Managing and mitigating errors in quantum computations.

Integration of Quantum Machine Learning in Industry:

Concept: The integration of QML into various industries will drive practical applications and real-world impact. Industry-specific use cases will showcase the benefits of quantum machine learning and contribute to its adoption.

Trends:

Healthcare: Applying QML to drug discovery, personalized medicine, and medical imaging.

Finance: Utilizing QML for portfolio optimization, risk management, and fraud detection.

Supply Chain: Enhancing logistics and supply chain management with quantum optimization and machine learning.

Applications:

Predictive Analytics: Improving predictive models for various industries.

Optimization: Enhancing optimization solutions for complex industrial problems.

Challenges:

Industry Adoption: Overcoming barriers to adoption and integrating QML into existing systems.

Cost: Managing the costs associated with quantum hardware and software.

Challenges in Quantum Machine Learning

Hardware Limitations and Scalability:

Concept: Quantum hardware limitations and scalability issues present significant challenges for the development and application of QML algorithms. Addressing these challenges is crucial for realizing the full potential of quantum computing in machine learning.

Challenges:

Qubit Quality: Ensuring high-quality qubits with low error rates and long coherence times.
Quantum Volume: Increasing the quantum volume to handle larger and more complex computations.
Resource Management: Managing the resources required for large-scale quantum computations.

Algorithm Development and Optimization:

Concept: Developing and optimizing quantum algorithms for machine learning tasks is a complex and ongoing challenge. Creating algorithms that are both effective and efficient requires significant research and development.

Challenges:

Algorithm Efficiency: Designing algorithms that achieve quantum speedup while remaining practical and efficient.
Training and Tuning: Optimizing quantum algorithms for specific machine learning tasks and tuning hyperparameters.

Data Handling and Preprocessing:

Concept: Handling and preprocessing data for quantum machine learning presents unique challenges due to the differences between quantum and classical data representations.

Challenges:

Data Encoding: Efficiently encoding classical data into quantum states for processing.
Data Preparation: Preparing data in a format suitable for quantum computations.

Integration with Classical Systems:

Concept: Integrating quantum machine learning systems with classical systems poses challenges related to interoperability and system design.

Challenges:

Hybrid Systems: Developing hybrid quantum-classical systems that leverage the strengths of both technologies.
Interface Design: Creating interfaces and protocols for seamless interaction between quantum and classical systems.

Future Directions and Research Opportunities

Advancing Quantum Algorithms: Continued research into quantum algorithms for machine learning will drive innovation and improve the effectiveness of QML techniques. Exploring new algorithms and refining existing ones will be crucial for advancing the field.

Enhancing Quantum Hardware: Advancements in quantum hardware will enable more powerful and practical quantum computations. Research into qubit technology, error correction, and hardware integration will be essential for supporting QML applications.

Addressing Real-World Problems: Applying QML to real-world problems and industry-specific use cases will showcase its practical benefits and drive adoption. Focusing on high-impact areas such as healthcare, finance, and logistics will be important for demonstrating the value of QML.

Interdisciplinary Collaboration: Collaboration between quantum computing researchers, machine learning experts, and industry professionals will be key to advancing QML and addressing its challenges. Interdisciplinary approaches will facilitate the development of innovative solutions and practical applications.

The future of Quantum Machine Learning is poised to bring transformative changes to the field of machine learning by leveraging quantum computing's unique capabilities. This chapter provides a comprehensive overview of future trends and challenges in QML, including the development of new algorithms, advancements in quantum hardware, and industry integration. Understanding these trends and challenges is essential for driving innovation and realizing the full potential of QML. As quantum technology continues to advance, it will play an increasingly important role in shaping the future of machine learning and solving complex problems across various domains.

This detailed chapter explores the future trends and challenges in Quantum Machine Learning, covering key developments, potential challenges, and research opportunities. It provides a thorough understanding of how QML is expected to evolve and the factors that will influence its advancement and practical applications.

Free Gift

Click on the link to aceess your free full four hours introduction to programming course

Introduction to Programming